C000253104

everybody
welcome

the course where everybody helps grow their church

Bob Jackson
and George Fisher

Members' Manual

CHURCH HOUSE
PUBLISHING

Church House Publishing
Church House
Great Smith Street
London SW1P 3AZ

ISBN 978 0 7151 4219 6

Published 2009 by Church House Publishing
Third Impression 2010

Designed and typeset in Ergo 10pt by Jordan Publishing Design,
Salisbury, Wiltshire

Printed in England by Halstan & Co, Amersham, Bucks.

Contents

Introduction

Why welcome?

I (Bob) have been the visiting preacher at literally hundreds of churches. Even if my wife arrives with me she tends to become invisible at the church door. All too often where I have been feted, my wife has been ignored from the moment she received a hymnbook to the moment she finished her coffee. I should add that my wife really enjoys meeting people. But in many churches nobody even takes the trouble to say 'hello' and find out. Almost invariably, if church leaders have told me in the vestry what a friendly church this is, then my wife will assuredly have been ignored – what they mean is they are so friendly with each other they have no inclination to befriend the stranger.

Most churches think they are a friendly church because church members are friendly with each other. We may not realize how unwelcoming we appear to the outsider. The sad truth is that 90 per cent of the people who try out our churches fail to join them. In many churches it is normal not to speak to newcomers. We are not usually openly hostile, we just ignore them and eventually they go away.

But churches that do welcome and befriend the stranger are creating the sort of growing, flourishing community Jesus wants his church to be.

Everybody Welcome is about making welcome central to all we do and the people we are. Just think what the impact would be if not 10 per cent but 25 per cent or even 50 per cent of the people who try out your church succeed in joining it!

Welcoming newcomers into the worshipping community is a ministry not just for the clergy or other leaders but for every member of every church.

Everybody Welcome is a course for every church-going Christian who believes that belonging to their church is good for them and can be good for others. The title indicates not only that everybody should be *made* welcome but also that everybody should *be* welcoming.

Everybody Welcome aims to change your church by three routes:

1 helping every individual to have a welcoming approach to newcomers. So it is important that as many church members as possible take part in the course.

2 identifying priorities for decision and change. At the end of the course the church council or other leadership group should identify priorities and then develop and implement an action plan for improving the church's welcome and integration of newcomers.

3 setting up a Welcome Team, whose specialist ministry is to help newcomers through to being contributing members.

Welcome as a growth strategy

I've been studying the factors involved in church growth for many years and have reached a most surprising conclusion. At least it surprises me, and I'm sorry now that I've been so slow on the uptake.

We sometimes overlook the fact that it is Jesus' own job to draw all people to himself (Matthew 16.18) and he is still doing his job. The main problem and opportunity for the growth of the church today is how well we who are already in the church welcome the people whom God is sending us to join the church. It is as surprisingly basic and simple as that.

I can actually demonstrate this for an average church mathematically with some simple algebra, but if you want that take a look at the Course Leaders' Manual!

Welcome and the gospel

The hospitality of our welcome is central to our Christian calling. The gospel is about unconditional acceptance into the Body of Christ. Peter learned this lesson in Acts chapter 10 when, having accepted lodgings in the particularly smelly house of Simon the Tanner, he was taught in a vision to accept Gentiles as well as Jews into the church.

Welcome ministry is part of our response to God's ministry of reconciliation that he shares with his church. 2 Corinthians 5.18 says: 'All this is from God, who reconciled us to himself through Christ and gave us the ministry of reconciliation.' There is huge power in effective welcome because it is the very expression of the gospel of reconciliation between God and humans, and between humans. The heart of the gospel is that all are called, all are included, all who ask to enter are allowed in to the kingdom of heaven. 'You are all sons of God through faith in Christ Jesus ... There is neither Jew nor Greek, slave nor free, male nor female, for you are all one in Christ Jesus' (Galatians 3.26,28).

In the world around we see alienation, isolation, division, barriers, people who are unwelcome here, there and almost everywhere. In the faithful Christian church it does not matter whether or not your face fits – we have a gospel of reconciliation, a core value of radical inclusivity, a community of welcome to all. Your welcome, your inclusion, is based not on what you can give but on what can be given to you. You are welcomed in by grace, flowing from the supernatural love that God and his church already have in their hearts for you.

If anyone did not deserve to be welcomed it was the prodigal son. He had betrayed his father, squandered his money and ruined his family's reputation. And yet, as the son skulked home in search of a servant's meal, the father, ever watchful, rushed out to embrace him while he was still a great way off. Such is the prodigious welcome of God the Father for all his children making the slightest gesture of return from afar to the warmth of his family home. And such should be the prodigious welcome of his church to all who glance in our direction.

So we know the marvellous gospel theory that 'all are welcome' in the Church of Jesus Christ. Some churches struggle with this, others offer such a welcome that all manner of people are drawn to Jesus Christ through their welcome and friendship. But none can be complacent.

So we know what we should be like even if we sometimes fall short of high standards. Often the reason we fall short is not our lack of willingness, our rebellion against the ministry of reconciliation, our resentment at the prodigals. It is our lack of confidence, our fear of straying out of our comfort zone, our awkwardness with the stranger, and preoccupation with our own needs or stress that breeds indifference to others.

On our weaknesses God has compassion and yet he calls us to grow strong. This is where *Everybody Welcome* comes in – this course is designed to help every church that aspires to gospel standards of welcome and hospitality to put them into everyday practice. We can be the communities God intends us to be if we put our hearts and minds

to the task, obeying and imitating the God of hospitality who welcomes every sinner to sit, eat and rejoice at his table.

Welcome and the big picture

The whole life of the church is bound up with its ministry of welcome and integration. It is central to how the local church fulfils Jesus' great commission – 'Go and make disciples of all nations' (Matthew 28.19). Making contact with people, befriending them, welcoming them into membership of the community of Christ and nurturing them into Christian discipleship can only be achieved when the quality of the life of the whole church measures up to the task in hand. This course is not about a small specialist ministry, it aims to bring new health and vitality to the whole of church life.

So it helps to see where every aspect of the course fits in to the overall picture. Church members go through a life-changing, church-changing process of discovering the life of the church then experiencing its worship then belonging to its community then contributing to its ministry. There are different aspects of each stage in the journey, and they are labelled and summarized in the chart below, which is our equivalent of a table of contents.

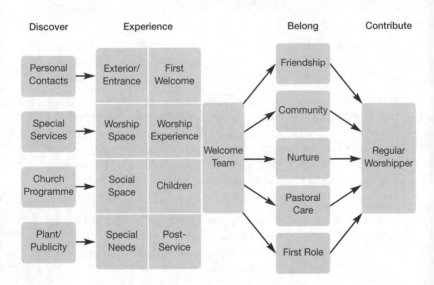

So *Everybody Welcome* is divided into four sessions:

Session 1. Helping people discover the church's existence and character

People have to at least know about you, and may well need to know you in person, before thinking of becoming part of your group. So how does your church make contact with the local community and how can you become more visible in it?

Session 2. Giving people a good experience of the church premises

The church grounds, building and hall can attract or deter people. So how daunting is the physical business of entering your building for the first time? Can you develop your facilities to provide a positive and anxiety-free experience?

Session 3. Giving people a good experience of the church people

A newcomer's first experience of the church community usually determines whether they wish to join it. So how can your church offer a friendly, stress-free welcome to the local community? But people need to experience divine welcome as well as human. So how can you best give newcomers the chance to meet with God in your worship and other community events?

Session 4. Helping newcomers belong to the church community and start contributing to it

Church attendance should be a step along the way to Christian discipleship. Most people aspire to belong, not just to attend. The main factor in deciding whether someone stays is whether they make friends quickly. So how can your church be motivated, trained and organized to offer attractive friendship and belonging to newcomers? How can newcomers turn into members who exercise their own Christian ministry through the church?

There is a fifth session, but this is for the setting up of a church 'Welcome Team' and so only the team members are needed to attend.

How *Everybody Welcome* works

You will find the outline for each 90-minute session later in this manual. As an example, Session 1 'Discover' is divided into four sections that reflect the four main ways in which people discover about the life and existence of a church – personal contacts, the church's regular programme, special services and events, and its premises and publicity. Each section has some introductory input to it, in this manual and in the session itself, some of it on DVD. Course members are then asked to respond by filling in a personal tick-box checklist and talking through one or two discussion questions in pairs or small groups. The personal checklists will be issued at the start of each session.

At the end of the session the group will know the average score for each section. This will reveal where you think your strengths and weaknesses lie. At the end of the whole course it should therefore be possible to work out priorities for change. How can the strengths be reinforced and the weaknesses tackled?

During the week before each session please read through the relevant part in the manual and spend some time praying and thinking about the theme and its implications for yourself and your church.

As you read the Members' Manual do note down your own ideas plus any sense of what God is saying to the church. These can be shared with others when you meet.

As with all things to do with the Christian life and church, our human efforts will be useless without prayer and without the work and power of the Holy Spirit. We believe that God the Holy Spirit has already been directing the Church towards improving its welcome and hospitality – we can see this through the progress of 'Back to Church Sunday', through our research into how churches are growing and shrinking and in the reactions to the drafts and trials of this course. We are catching God's agenda for the Church. So do please make praying for the success and impact of this course a personal priority! You may wish to use the Course Prayer inside the front cover of this manual on a regular basis.

Discover

Making the church more visible

■ Contents ■

Session 1 pre-reading

Discovery as a starting point

People will not join a church until they discover it. In order to have a chance of welcoming people to worship with us we first have to show them that a living and active church exists. It's surprising what people assume just from the look of the church building. If you board up the windows the vandals smashed, then the neighbours may assume the church is closed.

As well as the visibility of the church building, people discover a church through the activity of the church members. Churches need to live their lives visibly out in the open where others can discover their existence and begin to relate to them. Some churches have a low profile, very limited contact with their local community and, as a result, very few visitors. Others have a high profile, masses of contacts, a large fringe, and many people trying them out. What about your church?

There are four ways in which churches make contact with their local communities and we'll look at each in turn. Your assessment of the church's strengths and weaknesses in each area will reveal priorities for improvements and may also help you think through your own part in making the church more visible and attractive to the local community.

The four main ways of becoming visible are:

1 Personal contacts
2 The church programme
3 Special services and events
4 Church premises and publicity

1 Personal contacts

This is so obvious it is easy to overlook. So take a moment to think about how many family, friends, acquaintances, neighbours and colleagues you know who do not go to church. Some Christians have got so immersed in church over the years that they know hardly any people who are not already Christians. How ironic that faithful commitment to God's Church can suck Christians out of the very places where we are needed! It is also a disaster! Christians should not live in isolated ghettos but be salt in society, learning from and contributing to a wide range of other people.

If your church has so taken over your life that there is little else in it you may like to consider how to start making friends with non-churchgoers again.

Now use your instinct to draw up a shortlist of people you know that may just accept an invitation to come to a church service or event. For some of you the list may be very short indeed but make it anyway! Write down the number of people you have identified in the box below and bring it with you to Session 1.

Over to you ...

The number of people I can think of is:

A recent survey found out how many people in Britain say they would like to go (often, return) to church if only they were invited. The answer was three million! That's almost as many as those who go already. On average each churchgoer will know at least one other person who does not have the courage to go to church alone but is hoping to be asked by someone who already does go. But so far they haven't been asked. So one or two of the people you have thought of might actually be thrilled to be invited!

So the first and most important way of making a first contact is personal and involves every church member. People discover our churches through us inviting them in.

Sometimes the first invitation will be to a social event or some other element of the church's programme that is not an act of worship. Sometimes it is best simply to invite someone to a church service. This is what people expect us to be about, this is the heart of what we do and the best way to meet the church as a whole.

Proof of how effective personal contacts and invitation are is provided by 'Back to Church Sunday'. This new idea labels the last Sunday in September as 'Back to Church Sunday'. Invitation cards are given to church members with which to invite their contacts to church on the special day. In 2007 in the Diocese of Lichfield alone around 6,000 people accepted a personal invite from churchgoers and went to church with them. Six months later a repeat survey found that between 700 and 900 of the 6,000 were now regular churchgoers. A further 3,000 still retained a contact with the church and had probably been back at least once, perhaps at Christmas.

So whom should you invite to church with you one Sunday, perhaps as part of your church's next 'Back to Church Sunday'?

For most people a single invitation is not enough. Even if they come with you once it does not mean that they will now feel able to come under their own steam thereafter. Be sensitive and don't put someone off by overdoing things, but be prepared to invite people two or three or four or more times to services and events before they begin to feel sufficiently at home not to need further help.

2 The church programme

Churches offer all sorts of meetings, groups, events and services to their local communities. Collectively these can be called the church's 'programme' – the list of things the church does. Of course this list is often not the result of a fully thought-out strategy resulting in a coherent 'programme'. In many churches the list of what is done is more the piecemeal result of history. But let us call it the church's programme anyway!

Very often the programme is focused on community use of the church premises. Many churches have pre-school groups, pensioners' clubs, lunch clubs, youth clubs, open house cafes, or uniformed organizations meeting on their own premises. Many of these will attract members who do not attend regular church services.

There are two main routes into the worshipping community available for such people. One route is that the group they attend becomes a halfway house into church worship. A lady attends a lunch club and sits next to another lady who is a church member. They become friendly and she gets invited along one Sunday. Or else she is given an invitation card to a carol service, and, when she gets there, she is pleased to meet up with a couple of other lunch club members.

The other route is that the church takes steps to turn the event on the programme into 'church' for the people who attend it. For example, one church moved its weekday service to half an hour before the start of the lunch club. Most of the members started turning up half an hour early so that church worship, lunch and fellowship became part of the same event and experience. Another church held a regular Saturday morning men's breakfast with a speaker, some prayer and singing. Some of the men thought they were coming to a social event with a good cooked breakfast. But if it quacks like a duck and waddles like a duck, it's a duck. They had been to church.

Some churches turn their premises into a base for community action, perhaps calling it a 'social action centre'. The aim is simply to serve the local community but one outcome is usually that a lot more contacts are made. Many people are able to discover the life and people of the church through its community enterprise.

Many churches will also hire out their premises to all manner of community groups for events that are not part of the church's own programme but still take place on church premises. These at least get people used to coming to the church premises and they open up new contact and discovery opportunities. Churches where the worship space is multi-purpose and available to let during the week have a particular advantage here – the premises ice has been broken.

Some churches simply see these user groups as revenue sources. Some even make the mistake of taking so many bookings (in order to balance the books) that the church can't use its hall for its own events. Other churches see the user groups as contact points and take steps to get to know them. One church appoints a link person for every user group. Their job is to attend the group regularly, ensure smooth relationships between the group and the church, to befriend the members and introduce them to the wider life of the church.

In some churches the programme of community service will involve activities not based on the church premises at all. Examples include home visiting of the disabled and elderly people, gardening services to pensioners, debt advice, or charity fund-raising. One church has a large number of such 'touching points'. Three times a year it invites the contacts made to join an Alpha Course. Many people over the years have followed this route into faith starting with a touching point, then Alpha, then joining the worshipping community.

Some churches have an annual round of fund-raising social events that involve a lot of others in the local community – the Christmas Fayre, the Summer Fete etc. These can be good fun, draw the church together, and be great points of contact with others. The danger is that the church is seen as being mainly interested in other people's money to keep them going. But there is also a great opportunity to develop links, to get noticed and to enable people to take the next step. At such events there should always be an invitation to a future special church service or event.

Many churches have too big a programme. It is too burdensome and nothing is done very well. It exhausts the members trying to keep things going and they get de-motivated. A healthy church does a few things well. It concentrates on those that are the most effective today in forwarding the whole mission of the church: pastoral, evangelistic and social. What are your best opportunities for enabling people to get to know the church and the God who inhabits it?

Over to you ...

Which groups and activities in your church have brought new people into the worshipping community over the last few years? Where do you think there is potential in the future?

3 Special services and events

Some people discover a church through attending a special service or event. They may come along to the school harvest service their child is singing in, or to the crib service or Christingle or Midnight Communion.

Or maybe they come to the 'Christian' pantomime or a Mission Weekend event. Others may attend a 'memorial service' or a wedding or a baptism or a funeral.

There are three main questions to ask yourself about your church's special services. First, do you have an appropriate range of them? Second, do people who are not already church members actually come to them? Third, how clear and how well travelled is the route from attending a special service to becoming part of the regular congregation?

Try listing the special services your church has over the course of a year to which non-members regularly come. Then make a guess at how many people attend them in total. You might be quite surprised by the number. So, is your church one with a lot of special services and so a lot of contact with people, or one with few of these opportunities?

Creating such opportunities may be part of your strategy for meeting new people and welcoming them into the regular worshipping community. But how well done are your events and do they act as a good way in to the rest of church life? Church members are needed in some numbers at these events in order to talk to and befriend people. Memorial services have grown in popularity in recent years but they rarely result in people joining the regular congregation usually because they are held at a different time and the regular congregation don't come.

So there is a strong case for having special services or events at the normal service times to help those who attend the specials into the regular life of the church. If the special service is at its own time then it is important to have church members – especially the Welcome Team – present at it to make the connections for the visitors.

4 Church premises and publicity

What do your church grounds and buildings look like to outsiders? Do they have to hack their way through an overgrown graveyard to even glimpse the prison-like church door? Was it their Nan's funeral last time they came? If the buildings and grounds look unfriendly and are associated with negative feelings some people in your community will avoid them at all costs. Far too many of our buildings either say to the passer-by 'Closed' or 'Keep out'. One evening this week wander round your church grounds and buildings trying to see them with a stranger's eye. If possible bring along a friend or neighbour who does not attend church and ask them to tell you the images and feelings conjured up inside them. What could be done to improve things?

Other church buildings are a great asset to our welcome – they look beautiful and well cared for, places for meeting with God. If you are able to keep the church unlocked during the day then do everything you can to encourage people to come in to find some quiet space, to pray, or just to enjoy the building. Offer refreshments if you can.

Other people discover the church's premises by attending an event or group in the church hall. What does the state of the hall say about the church as a community? Is it well cared for and good quality or a bit of a mess? If money is an issue it is often possible to find grants and outside finance to improve a church hall that has wide community use.

Over to you ...

Try looking at your notice board with an outsider's eye, or else bring a friend to look at it. Does it convey the right information in language people will understand? What unspoken messages about the church does its style and condition convey?

Most people today if they are looking for a church will browse the web. Will they find your church if they do so? Every church should have its details somewhere on the web. Web sites need a webmaster to keep them up to date and attractive.

I went to a fresh expressions-style church recently. The evening began with a barbecue on the church steps, followed by an act of worship inside. I chatted over burnt sausages to one young man, who said it was his first time. 'How did you hear about it?' I asked. 'On Facebook', he replied.

So keep ahead of the game – what new communications tools could effectively publicize your church? The early church spread through using the cutting-edge communications technology of the day – the Roman road. What is the appropriate technology today for your church?

Ideas and links for web sites and other publicity and communications tools are available on our web site: **www.everybodywelcome.org.uk**

Electronic tools have not, however, entirely replaced the parish magazine. Who is your magazine for? The most effective are aimed at the whole local community. Let them be Christian in content and advertise the church's services and programme, but let them also be a useful tool for general community cohesion. If you can finance the magazine in some way, perhaps through adverts, and post it free through every letter box then so much the better.

But the magazine can be a turn-off. If prominently displayed is a long list of church office-holders and job vacancies it gives the Church the image of being an organization with servants trapped into onerous voluntary jobs. Post-moderns will run a mile. It may be more effective to circulate a church DVD on which a range of congregation members talk about their faith and the church, and on which clips of church services and events are shown. The overall message is not, 'Come and join our organization and become a treasurer or secretary of something', but 'We are on a spiritual journey, like you are. Come and relate with us as we go on our journey together.'

Leaflet drop invitations can still be effective, but be aware of the sheer amount of material that drops through letterboxes these days. The general experience is that people respond well to Christmas invitations but not at other times of the year.

■ Session 1 outline ■

Welcome Housekeeping notices and prayer .... 3 minutes

DVD Introduction and **The word on the streets** .... 4 minutes

Word on Welcome Reading: Acts 2.42–47 with
brief comment .... 6 minutes

Do we know anyone? Asking course members how many
people they know who might respond to an invite to a church
event or service .... 2 minutes

Personal contacts checklist Individuals tick boxes, discuss
in pairs or groups then hand checklists in .... 11 minutes

What goes on at our church? Compiling a list of the
elements of the church's programme .... 6 minutes

DVD A church at the heart of its community
St Edmund's Whalley Range, Manchester .... 7 minutes

The church programme checklist Individuals tick boxes,
discuss in pairs or groups then hand checklists in .... 9 minutes

What special services do we have each year?
Compiling a list .... 6 minutes

The special services checklist Individuals tick boxes,
discuss in pairs or groups then hand checklists in .... 9 minutes

DVD How do they do that? A church that raised its profile
Hope City Church, Sheffield .... 6 minutes

The premises and publicity checklist Individuals tick boxes,
discuss in pairs or groups then hand checklists in .... 9 minutes

So what did we learn? Sharing of ideas and conclusions,
announcing checklist results .... 10 minutes

DVD Authors' conclusion The two engines of change .... 1 minute

Course Prayer .... 1 minute

The premises

Making them more inviting

■ Contents ■

Session 2 pre-reading

In Session 1 we established that people experience your church's worship for the first time through a variety of routes.

But experience suggests that very few of those who 'try us out' actually stick and become regular congregation members themselves. When it comes to people who turn up for baptisms, weddings, funerals or carol services the percentage is nearly zero. How can we improve our welcome to worship so that more of the people who try attending end up belonging?

There are two dimensions of the initial experience of worship. One is physical and the other is human. Session 2 is about the easy bit – how welcoming is the physical environment a newcomer discovers? There are four main aspects of this:

1 Exterior and entrance

2 Worship space

3 Kitchen and social space

4 Provision for people with special needs

In each case the trick is to see ourselves as others see us.

1 Exterior and entrance

Many churches have had love and money lavished on them so they are attractive, welcoming buildings set in lovely grounds. They feel like a second home to the regulars but how do they seem to a newcomer?

One church had its grounds full of shrubs – vastly overgrown. The new vicar got a working party to clear the grounds and make lawns. One local resident responded, 'It's good to see it's open. We thought it had closed down.'

> **Over to you ...**
>
> Compare your church with a high street shop, a pub or restaurant.
>
> Go and stand outside some of them. How do you judge them from the outside? What makes you want to go in? Look at how much money they spend on making the entrance bright and attractive. Why do they think this is money well spent? How does your church compare?

The Diocese of Lichfield held a competition for the 'Worst Notice Board in the Diocese'. The prize was a new notice board. There were some spectacularly bad entries – if a shop had signage like that it would certainly get no customers. We'll show you some examples on the screen in Session 2. How good is your notice board?

I asked some church members what they thought of their church notice board. 'No idea' was the general answer – 'Do we have one, where is it?' Actually it was useless. But they didn't bother to check when they walked past it every week because they already knew the time and style of their own service and how to get hold of the vicar.

Sometimes we just don't see what sticks out a mile to an outsider.

2 Worship space

Are you worried about anxiety? When you open the church door and take a step inside do you emerge into an entrance hall or foyer dimly lit, smelling of something nameless, cluttered with stuff no one is brave enough to take to the tip and without clear directions to the next stage of the obstacle course called 'going to church'? Or do you walk straight into a warm, clean, well-lit worship space to be greeted by a smiling human being?

Buildings raise anxiety levels in people.

Anxiety levels are raised by:

- uncertainty – where do I go, what do I do when I don't know the house rules?

- clutter – feeling hemmed in, having to avoid it, being afraid of knocking something over

- feelings of not fitting in – I'm overdressed or underdressed for this environment, this is too posh or too down market for me

- smells, grot, litter, neglect, mystery, discomfort, dim lights, uneven floors, cold, poor signage

- unfamiliarity – 'I've never been in a place like this before', or 'It looks like a set from a horror movie.'

- staff who do not smile and do not offer to help.

A department store wants people to feel relaxed so they will enjoy spending their money and come back again. A good customer-care manager will patrol the store rooting out anything that raises anxiety levels. Assistants will help people find what they are looking for and take them to the appropriate department. Staff will be hired and fired on the basis not of skills but of attitude to customers. Could your church do with a customer-care manager?

Over to you ...

Does entering your church building raise anxiety levels in people who are not familiar with it? Ask around and chat to your friends. Make a note of any features that raise your anxiety level and hand it in to your course leader.

So, you have received a bucketful of books and papers from someone by the door. He or she may not have told you what to do next but you have correctly guessed you are expected to sit down on a pew. Wisely, you sit near the back so that you do not stick out like a sore thumb with everyone else's eyes studying the back of your neck and trying to guess why on earth you have come.

What is the building going to do to you over the next hour or so?

Is the church well enough lit and the print large enough for the average 70-year-old to read? Are poor readers going to feel foolish? If so, they probably won't return.

Are the newcomers in shirt-sleeves and the regulars in fur coats? Many people today do not even possess any warm clothing. Is the old reassurance that 'Many are cooled but few are frozen' actually good enough in this day and age?

When the warden of one church died, they found he had superglued the thermostat inside the boiler casing so no matter what you did with the dial the boiler stayed on 'low'!

One church needed the heating on for 36 hours to get warm and prevent down draughts that turned the pages for you. When they began to do this it was a great investment because people came, stayed – and *paid*!

Is the seating comfortable and attractive? Pew enthusiasts please consider whether you sit by choice on hard wooden benches in your living room at home and expect guests to do the same! I recently spent time helping Anglican churches in Australia think about how to grow. I sat in about ten churches. Having a slightly bad back, I could not have joined any of them because every dismal pew mangled my back. My sister came to my own church one Sunday for a healing service. She has a bad back, too. When the time came for people to go up for prayer the pew had done for her – she couldn't move!

Do newcomers run the risk of sitting in some regular's place and either offending them or being moved on? One couple came to a midweek service and were 'asked to move' three times! They refused to come back. I told the congregation that if that couple lost faith, then on Judgement Day they would have to face God with what they had done. But if they ever did it again they would have to face me first!

Is there a good-quality sound system such that everyone can hear the leader, preacher, notices, music group leader's introductions etc.? Is the sound level of the organ or the music group about right? The big amplification that excites younger ears can be painful to older ones.

Are the data projector and screen good quality and is the screen visible from every seat? A good system means people no longer have to locate hymn numbers in books, they sing looking up not down, the worship can flow from one song to another, you can use video clips and sermon illustrations, and the screen can welcome people and give simple notices that lower anxiety levels before the service begins. Fewer people read books these days, but everyone is used to watching a screen.

23

Do the notice sheets, hymn and service books make you proud to be a member of this church?

My bladder is still in reasonable working order, but churches without toilets will increasingly worry me as I get older. They certainly worried me when our children were young! 'What are we doing wrong?' asked one church. 'We do everything right but the young families never stay long.' They were expecting a sophisticated reply from the church growth expert. 'They won't stick until you get a toilet', I replied.

Are the signs to the toilet clear and visible and are the toilets clean, non-smelly, easily accessible without an embarrassing walk along the edge of the communion rail? Are there enough so there is no queue when the newcomer is likely to need them? Are there baby-change facilities and wheelchair access?

Finally, how does the building connect you with God, or at least calm you down and enable you to be in touch spiritually? The architecture of the internal space can depress or excite, lift you to the heavens or make you miserable. Some people respond spiritually to ancient Gothic buildings that have been prayed in for centuries. Others are turned off and need a human-scale hall. It is interesting that, usually, when a congregation has to leave its specialized church building for a few months for reordering or repairs, congregation numbers grow. They return to normal when the building is reoccupied. What dynamic is going on there?

Is it easy to pray in your worship space? Does it feel prayed in and loved? What do the wall hangings, statues, communion table, candles, kneelers, stained glass windows, pulpit, or cross over the archway do for you? Do you feel psychologically comfortable sitting in some places and not in others? Do you leave those less-favoured places for the strangers?

3 Kitchen and social space

At long last the service is over and you are invited to refreshments. This is the last and greatest hurdle of them all.

The first issue is information and invitation. It helps if the service leader has invited you to coffee. But he or she may not have told you where to go. The most important invite is personal – if a regular invites you to join them for refreshments you are likely to go, if not you may slip away fast. In many churches newcomers are genuinely welcomed to refreshments at the end, but not everywhere!

I visited one church that had seen rapid attendance decline. 'We only serve refreshments to the regulars when the others have gone', explained the warden. She indicated a secret area behind a curtain. 'The new people just shake hands with the vicar on the way out.'

Another church had seen a lot of new people. Over coffee in the hall a newcomer wandered in as a regular was overheard to say, in a loud stage whisper, 'Not another bloody newcomer.'

So are your newcomers genuinely made to feel welcome to socialize at the end of a service?

If refreshments are served very close to the worship area within the same building more people will join in than if they are served in a church hall a short walk away going outdoors. Are you serving refreshments in the right place and, if not, could you?

If refreshments are not served this may mean there is no community to invite newcomers to join. If the regulars scuttle off at the blessing without chatting to each other, what chance is there of them welcoming strangers?

What do you do if your church is small and you cannot install a kitchen? You might remove the back pew to create a circulating space and install a bench on which to boil a kettle and put out some attractive biscuits. One church made the furniture for their new refreshment point out of the back pew timber – neat eh! Or bring large flasks of hot water. There is always a way if there is a will.

Is the kitchen clean, modern, hygienic, well designed for largish-scale catering, with plenty of space and no health and safety issues? Are you legally allowed to sell food to the public from it? When was it last inspected? Or is it the sort your grandma used to have? Is there a constricted serving hatch that generates a huge queue just for a cup of tea? Would you be happy if the church kitchen were your own kitchen at home?

The content of refreshments offered is important. Tastes have become more sophisticated and quality assumed as a right. But some churches still offer bottom-of-the-range coffee and biscuits, and many even charge for them. Any church serious about welcome and hospitality will have a budget for refreshments and offer them for free. The food and drinks will be high quality and fairly traded.

It was 'Back to Church Sunday' at St Agatha's. Guests had come and the church had gone to town with the biscuits – top of the range instead of the usual chocolate-free zone. A visitor really fancied a chocolate biscuit and asked for one at the hatch. 'I'm sorry, they've been very popular and they've all gone,' said the serving lady, 'I had to save mine on the side here.' Which all goes to prove it is easier to solve the physical problems of the building than the human ones!

What happens after the service can be a major part of the experience for children as well as adults. Do the refreshments offered to children make them feel special and want to come again? Is the aim to save money on their refreshments or to make the children happy? If the church is still offering junk food what are the healthy options to move towards?

At the end of a service children prefer to play with each other rather than stand around a hall listening to adults gossip. Where can they go and what can they do? I once built a model railway that came out to be played with when the church service was over. We had a balcony from which we held paper aeroplane competitions using old notice sheets. We let the smaller children play with the drum kit provided they didn't hit it too hard! And we always displayed their craftwork. The church I was at the other week brought out the table tennis table at the end of the service and I much preferred playing with the teenagers than standing around being polite with the adults!

What is there in your church to make the children feel at home and want to return because they feel special and have fun?

Our health and safety culture has its idiocies, but how safe is your church, kitchen, social space, church path, car park and grounds? If parents spot sharp points protruding from old metal chairs, or dangerously hot radiators, or broken glass, or plain honest dirt, or they are nervous about fire precautions, they may not bring their tiny tots again.

A well-cared-for, safe, high-quality environment for refreshments, socializing and playtime is no substitute for welcoming human beings. But it certainly helps!

4 Provision for people with special needs

Making provision for people with special needs is not a matter of offering optional extras for small minorities but of maintaining the essential features of a welcoming church.

My Mum was 96 and couldn't see as well as she did. Churchgoing was stressful because she couldn't read the words in most hymn books and join in properly. One Sunday friends took her to a different church where she asked for a large-print hymn book. 'We can do better than that', they said, giving her the full order of service including all the liturgy, hymns and notices in a really clear large-print folder. She could join in with no trouble and loved the welcome she had been given.

Most of us do not have to wait until we are 96 to have some sort of special need or weakness that makes a significant difference to our experience of the worship event. Here is a far from exhaustive list:

- Bad back – I put this first because it's personal!
- Hard of hearing
- Find loud noises from organs or music groups distressing
- Deaf
- Need reading glasses and find small print hard
- Colour blind
- Blind or partially sighted
- Wobbly on feet, use a stick, elderly
- Wheelchair user
- Disabled badge holder
- Not fully confident of the bladder (applies to the very young as well as to elderly people)
- Bald – in trouble from those overhead radiant heaters some churches have unthinkingly installed (this too is personal!)
- Food allergies
- Recovering alcoholic (communion wine problems)
- Need to breast-feed
- Tabloid-only reader
- Illiterate
- English as second language

- Little or no English
- Very short – mainly but not exclusively children
- Very tall
- Overweight – some pew spaces and chairs are embarrassingly inadequate for what is known in church circles as 'the wider community'
- Dodgy knees – to kneel or not to kneel, that is the question
- Short attention spans – mainly applies to children but to plenty of others as well!

It is no use saying we don't have anyone with a particular special need so we don't need to provide for it. Usually people will only start coming once they are provided for!

I met Fred at the hospital where his wife was dying: both of them were profoundly deaf. Elsie died and two weeks later Fred came to church with an interpreter. We had to allow the service to be interrupted. The following week he brought two friends and the following week two more (all deaf). The interpreter and his wife both became Christians, and trained over twenty others to sign for all the deaf people who had joined our congregation because we had provided for their needs.

Over to you ...

Probably the majority of your congregation have some sort of special physical need or issue that affects their church experience. On the list above tick any that affect you, or perhaps a friend. Add any I missed out. How well does your church cater for your special need and how could it improve? If you have a suggestion or request to make, write it down and bring it to Session 2. Hand it to the course leader.

■ Session 2 outline ■

Exercise on arrival Seeing the building with new eyes followed by a 5 minute break before the start of the session .... **allow up to 30 minutes**

Welcome Housekeeping notices and prayer .... **3 minutes**

DVD Introduction Getting worried about anxiety and **Out and about: Photos of unwelcoming churches** .... **3 minutes**

Word on welcome Reading: Matthew 21.12–16 with brief comment .... **6 minutes**

Strangers' report How welcoming they find your premises? ... **8 minutes**

DVD Customer Care in the church Mark Hope-Urwin compares customer care in the retail sector and church .... **7 minutes**

What did you notice? Those who tried to see the building with new eyes before the session started report what they saw .... **8 minutes**

Checklists Exterior and entrance; worship space; social space; special needs – fill in, discuss in pairs or groups and hand in .... **35 minutes**

DVD How do they do that? How churches can make thier buildings welcoming during the week .... **8 minutes**

So what did we learn? Sharing ideas and conclusions, announcing checklist results .... **10 minutes**

DVD Authors' conclusion What are you going to do? .... **1 minute**

Course Prayer .... **1 minute**

A welcoming God

Session 3

and his welcoming people

■ Contents ■

Session 3 pre-reading

The bishop and his wife were returning from their package holiday one Sunday morning. Driving from the airport they entered the diocese. 'I know,' said the bishop, 'Let's drop in at St Mary's on the way home, we're just in time.' At 10.25 they walked into St Mary's in their holiday clothes, collected their hymn books and sat on the next to the back pew, bowing their heads in prayer. The churchwarden came up and whispered, 'I'm sorry you can't sit there, that's Mrs Jones's pew.' The bishop looked up, startled. The churchwarden said, 'Oh my God. It's the bishop!' She then insisted that the bishop and his wife could stay in Mrs Jones's pew after all, but this just made the bishop even crosser.

After the service the bishop and the churchwarden went for a walk together, circling the outside of the church building. The warden explained that she was very afraid of the scene Mrs Jones would make if someone else occupied her sacred seat. The bishop explained that most newcomers, asked to move, would walk straight out even before the service began. The warden kept muttering forlornly, 'We've got to change, haven't we bishop, we've got to change. We've got to change ...'

We have looked at the physical aspects of the church's welcome to newcomers. Now we turn to the even more important human aspects. Most people come to church to develop relationships – both with God and humans. But human behaviour is harder to change than physical buildings – people have wills of their own! It only takes one person out of a congregation of a hundred to mess up the welcome to a newcomer. However, the Christian faith is all about being changed and sanctified by God, so change is entirely possible and its rewards are great. Let's start with the initial welcome as churchgoers arrive for the worship event ...

1 Initial welcome

The initial welcomer (sidesperson in Anglican churches) is a key individual in the whole welcome ministry. First impressions can win or lose a new member.

Sometimes the job seems to be all about handing out the hymn book, prayer book, order of service leaflet, notice sheet, the hymn book supplement for the hymn written in 1964, the invitation to the parish weekend, the card with Easter services printed on, the extra sheet of paper with the *really* modern song written in 1988, and the appeal for funds to replace the clapped-out photocopier.

If possible, this great pile is landed on you without eye contact. In one church, resourceful sidespeople so positioned the table loaded with these goodies that their backs faced the entrance. They then perfected the art of handing the bundle to incoming worshippers backwards over their shoulders without at any time actually having to see their faces.

Once as a new vicar I was bemused by the sidespeople. They were different every week and I had no idea who they were. Eventually I discovered the church had found a way to attract non-members to come along. They were put on the sidespeople's rota and turned up three times a year to welcome people in. In most churches the regulars welcomed the strangers. In this church it was the other way round.

The main role of sidespeople is not to hand stuff out, but to make everyone feel welcome and at ease. For a newcomer the arrival moment is the point of acutest anxiety. It is the moment of opening wide and seeing the dentist's drill descend. If the dentist is human, smiling, and reassuring, if she explains what she is doing and tells you it won't hurt, then your anxiety level goes down. If she just comes at you with a drill you panic.

It is a good idea to have one sidesperson outside, welcoming people before they set foot in the building. People who look unsure can be accompanied in and shown the ropes. Those at a loss for where the entrance is, or who are having an attack of nerves, can be greeted and given confidence. If it is raining equip welcomers with very large umbrellas under which to walk people in.

It is also a good idea to have enough folk on duty to spare one to accompany newcomers or people with particular needs to good seats and get them settled, to explain what is going to happen, and to answer questions. If a newcomer is spotted the sidesperson should know who in the congregation it is safe to sit them next to. 'Hello Sam, this is Joyce and Geoffrey, they're new so would you mind if they sit with you and you showed them the page numbers?'

Most people genuinely want to be welcomed, but a few individuals just want anonymity. The fear of being too pushy compounds our natural shyness so that we make avoiding 'over-welcome' an excuse for not properly welcoming anyone. It is usually obvious if someone does not want warm human contact, and sidespeople need enough sensitivity to spot them. But the fall-back behaviour pattern must be warmth and welcome.

An elderly lady arrived at church for the first time. The sidesperson shook her hand and said, 'Welcome to St Mary's.' The lady burst into tears and the sidesperson wondered what he had done wrong. After they had sat the lady down and dried her tears she explained, 'That is the first time anyone has touched me for three years.' A simple human gesture had overwhelmed her. Do not underestimate the impact of human warmth and contact on the isolated and lonely victims of shattered communities and broken families who live all around us.

Many newcomers assess whether they stand a chance of joining a church within seconds of entering the door. There is one key question – 'Is there anyone like me?' So have a range of people and ages on the sidesperson's rota. If the aim is to attract families to this service then families should be on the front line of welcome. If teenagers, then teenagers. If pensioners, then pensioners.

Some churches issue name badges to the initial welcomers. This identifies their role and helps newcomers relate to them – so their use should be encouraged. These can also be a way of finding out who visitors are. 'Hello, as you can see, my name is Richard, welcome to All Saints. I don't think we've met, have you been before?' is likely to elicit at least a name in response. That name should be committed to memory, written down and used again the very next time a newcomer returns.

How big should the rota of welcomers be? Most people today do not wish to be tied down every week, or even most weeks, to a regular job in a church. Perhaps an ideal mix is to have four or five teams or individuals all on once a month, but one or two people (perhaps an overall leader of the team) who will be ever-present and able to spot those who have already come once or twice.

Welcomers or sidespeople should smile easily, be relaxed in company, sensitive with others, and motivated not only to draw other people into the fellowship of the church and the love of God that they themselves value. If you are not one already, could this be for you?

Welcomers should arrive early and have the piles of stuff all sorted before most people arrive. That way they can concentrate on the human relations. The table where the books are placed should not be behind the sidespeople so that their backs are to the people arriving when they sort and pick up the books. The table should not be between the sidespeople and the incoming worshippers as it then acts as a barrier. It should be to the side so that it is easy to shake hands and maintain eye contact throughout the initial welcome. If a table can be avoided altogether, so much the better.

It is preferable if there is actually very little to give out anyway. Dumping a pile of books and leaflets on a newcomer can raise anxiety levels right at the start. People are not used to finding hymn numbers or places in prayer books. If hymns and liturgies must be written out, it is usually worth the trouble of compiling them together in a single order of service that most strangers can follow reasonably easily.

Often today it's better to have most things on the screen using the data projector. A single attractive notice sheet is all that is needed to provide the opportunity for a warm human welcome.

2 The worship event

We have a lot to say about this, the centrepiece of the life of the worshipping community that we welcome people into. If you watch your local football team, the standard of the ground and whether the stewards welcome you in a civil manner and the quality of refreshments are important. But essentially you have come for the game itself. A dull 0–0 draw and you might not return. An exciting 4–3 win and you may be hooked!

By and large, if the church services just feel like a dull human activity no amount of community warmth will cover that up. But people will keep returning, blossom and grow, if they perceive that church worship enables genuine encounter with the living God.

We have so much to say about this that we can't squeeze it into the manual, so:

Over to you ...

There is a web site associated with this course – **www.everybodywelcome.org.uk** When you have found it click on 'worship event' and read all about it there! If you are not online then persuade someone to print off a copy for you. Or perhaps there may be copies available in church.

Just to whet your appetite, here are the headings for the material you will find there:

Good leadership

Service leaders need to be confident, clear and sincere. Care should be taken to help people through the especially stressful parts of the service like the Peace and receiving communion.

Good structure

Visitors need to know roughly what is going on and how long it is going to last or anxiety levels will go through the roof.

Good sermons

Most people still prefer a good sermon to a short one. Bad sermons can put people off, good ones can draw them into the heart of God.

Good music

Quality matters more than style but sincerity more than professionalism. We get a lot of our theology from the hymns and songs. They should be chosen thoughtfully.

Genuine warmth

Cold formality will not attract many people into the arms of the living God. How can I be a spiritual radiator rather than a refrigerator?

Accessibility

Some people respond spiritually to a cultivated sense of awe, wonder and mystery. But that is not the same thing as being unclear about what is going on. Most people will respond better if they know roughly what is happening.

Gospel-richness

Some Christians think we should go easy on 'Jesus' language with newcomers in case it puts them off. Usually it is Jesus who attracts and the Church that puts people off. Take people to the gate of heaven and they are likely to return for more.

Connecting with culture

Have you ever left a worship event feeling you weren't allowed to be 'yourself' or that the worship made little or no connection with the world you know? Worship should spark within the contemporary world, in the midst of the life and culture people know.

Doing things with a generous spirit is important. People pick these things up. Newcomers will tell if we'd rather be reading the Sunday papers with a big mug of coffee.

Trinitarian focus

Trinitarian worship helps communicate God's nature and character. Faced with a fuller understanding of Father, Son and Holy Spirit, newcomers as well as old hands will be more able to respond to him in worship.

All involved

Church worship tends to favour those with a verbal learning style, providing texts to read, speak, hear or sing. Perhaps it is time to redress the balance a little.

Creativity

For many, creativity is freedom, for others it feels like chaos. What is needed is a healthy framework within which our creative freedom can flourish.

3 Welcoming the children

Inviting, welcoming, retaining, nurturing and discipling children in the Christian church and faith is not just a job for specialists – it is the responsibility of the whole church community. The Church is always one generation away from extinction. Our main responsibility is to offer to

God new adults who will be the Christian witnesses and leaders for the next generations.

The principal failure of the Church in recent decades has been our failure to invite, welcome, integrate, nurture and disciple the children. This is also the principal threat to the existence of churches in the future – most adult Christians have a church background as children. How can we attract as adults generations who have known nothing of church all their lives? A church composed increasingly of elderly people is a church that has abandoned the children or else the children have abandoned it. Absence of children is also the principal blight on the happiness of churches today – churches with no children or young people are unhappy remnants, in mourning for a lost future.

One vicar told me – 'We don't cater for teenagers in this church because we don't have any.' What comes first, the chicken or the egg? If our church stopped catering for adults then before long we would have no adults either!

One good way of working out the priorities of churches is to look at their budgets. Jesus said, 'Let the children come to me, do not hinder them.' Yet the majority of churches have a bigger budget for church flowers than for the whole children's and youth ministry. How would we defend that at the Day of Judgement?

But it does not have to be like that! Some churches still come alive with the laughter of children and the energy of teenagers. Other churches, bereft of children for years, are learning to include them again. In some dioceses we have learned to invest in children and young people, and there are once again increasing numbers in the churches. As with adults, the key is how the existing church members welcome the children and invest their time, love, expertise, prayer and money in them. And if lots more children start coming along then the church will never be the same again. So what is our priority – keeping the style of church and worship we are comfortable with, or sharing the love of the Lord Jesus Christ with the children?

The Leaders' Manual contains a set of options for how churches today can invite, welcome and integrate children and teenagers into their life. In some churches it may be appropriate to have these notes copied round the course members so that you can get together for an extra session just to consider how you can improve your hospitality and facilities for the coming generations.

4 Caring for people after the service

The few minutes after the end of the service can be the most testing and crucial of all for a newcomer or visitor or fringe church member. During the service you can relax because nothing much is expected of you. But now there is the possibility of people coming up to talk to you, or, worse, of being ignored. Most people who try out a church and are not talked to at the end of the service will not come again. At maximum they will give it one more try.

Sometimes nobody speaks to the newcomer because the church is not organized and no individual thinks it is their responsibility. If nothing else comes of this course in your church it will have been worthwhile if everyone now recognizes it is their own responsibility to welcome and be hospitable to newcomers. That probably needs to be said and agreed at a church meeting so that everyone knows it is their responsibility to talk to strangers.

But also, in all but the smallest churches, it is important to have a specialist 'Welcome Team' with a particular remit for encouraging those appearing on the edge of church life to come into the centre of its community and ministry. The Welcome Team's role is to keep an eye on new people, introduce them to folk they might get on well with, make sure they are followed up, and encourage them through one or more of the routes into belonging we'll be dealing with in Session 4. Session 5 is designed as an initial training session for a Welcome Team.

■ Session 3 outline ■

Welcome Housekeeping notices and prayer .... 3 minutes

DVD Introduction A friendly church? and
Out and about: Finding the God moments .... 4 minutes

Word on welcome Reading: James 2.1–10 with brief
comments .... 6 minutes

DVD What mystery worshippers say .... 7 minutes

Our mystery worshippers A report from those who
attended your own church as mystery worshippers .... 6 minutes

DVD How do they do that? Interview with Tim Lomax
about worship that works .... 7 minutes

Checklists Initial welcome; worship experience; children
and teens; after the service – fill in, discuss in pairs or groups
and hand in .... 35 minutes

True story A church member tells the story of how they
met a welcoming God and his welcoming people when they
first started coming to church .... 5 minutes

So what did we learn? What have we learnt from the
checklists (announce the results)? What are our strengths,
weaknesses and opportunities for change .... 15 minutes

DVD Authors' conclusion People will join a church if they
meet a welcoming people and are helped to encounter the
living God .... 1 minute

Course Prayer .... 1 minute

Belonging

to the church community

■ Contents ■

Session 4 pre-reading

If you put this session into practice, you will not only help the newcomers, you will improve the whole of church life!

Session 1 was about how to help people discover the church by making it more visible. Sessions 2 and 3 were about giving people a good initial experience of the church premises and the church people. Now you come to the hardest part. How can newcomers who had a positive experience of attending your church event or service start belonging to your church community? There are five main routes into belonging:

1 Personal friendship

2 Community life

3 Christian nurture

4 Pastoral care

5 Christian service

Through opening up these routes we are trying to make a reality of the church ideal that Paul describes in his letters:

> **Consequently, you are no longer foreigners and aliens, but fellow citizens with God's people and members of God's household.**
>
> *(Ephesians 2.19)*

> **So in Christ we who are many form one body, and each member belongs to all the others.**
>
> *(Romans 12.5)*

We are not here looking at first contact and initial welcome but at what happens in the weeks and months that follow. When we think of the word 'church' we often think of 'worship' or 'preaching', but for most new people what's important is 'belonging' and 'togetherness'. Church growth experts, Bob and Mary Hopkins, were once asked what they considered to be the most important factor in church growth. Their answer was, 'Glue! – whatever makes people stick.'

The nature of the glue may vary, but churches with good glue tend to grow. Sadly, in many churches, there is insufficient glue and people slip away, almost without being noticed. Imagine moving to a new area and attending a church for three or four weeks and then going missing to see what happened. Would anybody notice? What does happen after a few weeks when someone is no longer 'new' and not made a fuss of? This session is about developing a sense of belonging that enables faith to grow. It's about how to apply the glue that turns new attenders into members of the Body of Christ.

As you look at these materials keep in mind people you know who are new to church or use these four case studies to help to focus your thoughts:

Trish is a young single woman who has started to attend church. She has lots of problems and tends to tell people her troubles. At first they are attentive and caring but after a few weeks she finds that people are avoiding her. After a while she stops coming – people notice but breathe a sigh of relief!

Andy and Gina had a new baby and enjoyed coming to church a few times. People played with the baby and were friendly to them. But no one wanted to be pushy so Andy and Gina hardly learned anyone's names and were never invited to anything else. When the baby began teething and they lost a lot of sleep they drifted away from coming and nobody seemed to mind. When they went to book the baptism for their second child they were nervous of what the vicar would say.

Flo is a recently bereaved widow. She has lost her self-confidence but used to go to church and now comes to find solace. She doesn't stay at the end of the service as she cannot face people. She's not sure what she's looking for and gradually finds other things to fill her time.

Stan has been coming to church for a few weeks. He's really enjoyed the services and is thinking of joining the course he's been invited to. He got the flu and was off work and missed church for two weeks. Then he had to visit family and so it's now three weeks since he's been. What will people think? What will they say? He's not sure of what the reaction will be so hesitates to come and misses a fourth week, and a fifth ...

1 Personal friendship

Mrs Smith tried a church for the first time and, over coffee afterwards, a regular said to her, 'It's a very friendly church here.' Mrs Smith retorted: 'I don't want a friendly church. I want a church where I can make friends.'

For a newcomer, the fact that church members are friendly with each other is irrelevant; what counts is whether they are prepared to make friends with them. If someone makes a few friends in a church in the first few weeks they will stay, if not they won't.

Over to you ...

Do newcomers find it easy to make friends in your church? Ask the newer people at church about their experience. Even better, ask someone who tried the church out but didn't stick.

So if you are getting to know a newcomer but realize you are not going to be a natural friend for them, introduce them to other church members who may be. Perhaps they are at a similar life-stage, or live nearby, or have shared interests or sense of humour. Involve others in the business of offering friendship. If you invite the new people round to your house you might also invite a few other church members as well. If you invite the new chap to go to the football match with you, you may wish to take along another church member as well.

One of the first steps in belonging to the Body of Christ is to make friendships with other believers. The circles of friendships in churches are often very close. Are we prepared to open up our circle to include new people? This is the challenge of hospitality – making room for the new

41

person. It will mean change, and is costly, but in the end it is one of the most enriching aspects of church life.

2 Community life

Most churches have active social programmes through which new members can become part of the family of the church. It's something many churches are really good at and need to make the most of. Have you noticed how often new people come along to the social events?

> **Over to you ...**
>
> **List your church's social events. How suited are they to newcomers? What other events could you try?**

We moved to a new village and someone said, sniffily, 'I hope they'll come to the community centre social.' Our friend said, 'Have you invited them?' 'Oh no!' came the answer. Even though we saw a poster advertising it we didn't feel we could gatecrash uninvited so of course we didn't go!

It is vital to invite new people to your event; don't just rely on a poster or a slot in the notices. Personal invitation always works best. Some may say, 'I invite people but they never come.' Perhaps you need to go out of your way and say, 'I'll call for you and go with you.' Above all, be friendly! Even if we put on all the right events if we don't befriend people through them they will not stick!

3 Christian nurture (growing in faith)

> **Evelyn walked up to the vicar with a beaming smile. She had just completed the new 'beginners' course' and wanted to tell him how good it was. 'I've learnt more about Christianity in the last ten weeks than in all those sermons in the last three years!' she announced. He didn't know whether to be pleased or not!**

We don't want people simply to attend church, we want them to come to faith in Christ and grow in faith – 'To grasp how wide and long and high and deep is the love of Christ' (Ephesians 3.18).

Over to you ...

Read Paul's prayers for the church in Ephesians 1.17,18 and 3.16-21 and make them your ambition for the people of your church both old and new.

But spiritual growth does not happen automatically. People tend to take several years coming to a full Christian faith. We all need plenty of opportunities to learn about the faith, ask our questions and make our response.

Chris started attending church through meeting the curate's wife on an Open University Course. We were rejoicing a few months later when she responded to a call in a service to commit her life to Christ. But when she gave her testimony a few years later, I was astounded that the date she gave for committing her life to follow Christ was 18 months after the date when we had all rejoiced!

In the past many people had a good grounding in the Bible and the Christian faith. This gave them a head start when they decided to be practising Christians. Today, many people know very little about Christianity, not even the basic Bible stories or the Lord's Prayer. We must provide more help and information to enable people to make their decision whether to follow Christ and to equip them to live the Christian life. This is where the nurture course, or Christian basics courses, such as Alpha, Emmaus and Start! come in.

Many churches have found nurture courses invaluable not only for helping people explore the faith but also for helping them grow key friendships. There is nothing new about these courses. We have been doing confirmation courses and membership courses for ages. Today, however, we have people who wish to explore the Christian faith but are not ready to make the commitment to the church that confirmation and other membership courses entail. Nurture courses provide a place to explore questions of faith without demanding commitment to the church.

There are courses to suit a whole range of different churches and church traditions. They have been packaged to provide excellent materials in an accessible way. Most of them give helpful advice on how to set up a nurture group and run the course.

The Achilles heel of most nurture courses is what happens afterwards. Too often course members are simply expected to attend church services and no other guidance or provision is made. Alternatively, sometimes course members are bludgeoned to attend something else and feel pressurized. Each course participant should be given an opportunity to discuss their own personal next step. It is important to have something for those who wish to explore Christianity further. Some churches have a range of midweek fellowship groups or cell groups to offer to those who have completed the course. Other churches run a follow-on course, either another nurture course that complements the first one, or a course that looks at developing areas of faith. This can then, in time, become an ongoing fellowship or cell group. Some may want to do the course again, and often gain more from doing it a second time, but beware of those who never move on. Some will have done enough for the moment and it is important to allow them the freedom to end their involvement at this stage.

4 Pastoral care

Marie had been attending church for a few months. Since she came to the carol service and was clearly touched by God she has hardly missed a week though her husband never came. Then someone noticed she was missing for three weeks. She hadn't made many friends in church yet and so I went to visit, unsure of what sort of reception I would get. Something had happened to a friend and she'd hit a crisis of faith but we were able to talk it through and pray. Next Sunday she returned and before long her husband started coming. If I'd not done that visit ...

There are many stories similar to Marie's but how many stories are there that we know nothing about because the person has slipped away unnoticed? Once we start to come to church this is only the beginning of our journey of faith. Far too many people fall away after the first few weeks, or the first few months. The Parable of the Sower (Matthew 13.1-9) makes it clear that some will slip away but this is not an excuse for poor pastoral care. It is not enough simply to put the name and number of your 'pastoral coordinator' on the weekly notice sheet – every church member is needed to care pastorally for others.

Some people still think it is the minister's job to visit everyone, along with everything else! But gone are the days of the local parish church with one minister for 300 houses – if it ever existed. If effective pastoral care is to take place then it is everyone's responsibility. The very best pastoral care flows naturally from loving, caring relationships and never underestimate how much of this does happen in our churches. However, no congregation is perfect and people do get missed out. This is especially true of the newer people into church who have not fully become part of the church family.

Churches have tried all sorts of ways to improve their pastoral care. These are best considered as 'safety nets' to catch those who, for one reason or another, do not get picked up by the natural love and care of the congregation. In no way are they to be seen as replacing spontaneous love and care. Here are some of the different pastoral safety nets which churches have developed:

- pew pastors
- small groups (this can include the choir, Mothers' Union, and cleaning team, as well as fellowship groups)
- attendance registers
- alphabetical grouping.

Over to you ...

Refer back to the four case studies on page 40. How would these people be nurtured and pastorally cared for in your church? How would you try to stop them (and others) leaving your church?

5 Christian service

In most churches there is a small active group who do most of the work – church being like a passenger liner where a small crew work hard at making life pleasant for all the passengers.

All Christians are called to serve others and to use their gifts for the sake of the whole church. It is important for every congregation member, new and old, to develop and grow in Christian service. In this consumer society, how do we help people to become contributing crew members who talk about 'our church' rather than 'this church'?

In our present culture, 'commitment' is a dirty word. People are reluctant to commit themselves to a weekly (or even monthly) activity. Lifestyles have changed over the last 25 years and now people are often away at weekends visiting relatives or going on weekend breaks. In the past there was an army of housewives who took up all types of voluntary roles but they are now either working or looking after the grandchildren (or great-grandchildren!). This has affected not only the Church but many voluntary organizations as well.

As a result many churches are struggling to find people to fill the roles needed to maintain the work. It is therefore very tempting when someone new arrives to think in terms of 'What can we get this person to do?'

There are two different ways of approaching this. One group says, 'Give 'em a job to do as soon as possible, then they feel part of everything. That's the best way to keep them!' The other says, 'Don't scare people off by instantly pouncing on them to do a job no one else is willing to do. Get to know them, let them grow in trust and spirituality before using them!' Well, those are two opposing philosophies. Both have points to commend them and drawbacks.

Julia was asked to take charge of the reading rota. She had been in the church for quite a while and knew most people so she seemed ideal. The church didn't count on the fact that Julia had a heart for the outsider and she asked all the new people to do the readings. The long-standing church members were incensed – being asked to do a reading was a sign of being fully a member, not for newcomers. 'Exactly!' thought Julia.

Christian service is not just, or even primarily, about having a job in the church. It is about living Christianly out in the world. For some people, belonging is not enhanced through taking a job in the church but through being supported by the church in their demanding lives outside it. Individuals vary. That is why it is good practice, when someone has been coming to church for a little while, for the minister or another designated leader to have a private discussion with them about how they would like to develop their membership and contribution.

Over to you ...

Does giving new people a job to do keep them or drive them away?

Conclusions: keeping growing

We hope that you can now see what a vital area 'welcome' is and that through this course you have been able to see areas where change is needed.

What can you do personally to be more welcoming? It is only as each and every member of the church becomes more welcoming that the culture of the church will change. Remember, people do not simply want a 'friendly church', but a church where they can make friends. Each individual helps to provide the glue that helps people attach to a place and its people.

You will also have identified areas where changes need to be made in the church. Pray for your leaders as they seek to implement these changes and encourage them as you see developments taking place.

We hope and pray that this course will help your church to be more effective in its welcome so that new people who try you out will stay and so discover the welcoming heart of God.

■ Session 4 outline ■

Welcome Housekeeping notices and prayer .... 3 minutes

DVD Introduction Belonging: the glue that helps people to stick and **People talking: What makes you feel you belong?** .... 4 minutes

Word on welcome Reading: Ephesians 2.19 and Romans 12.5 with brief comment .... 5 minutes

Interview with two course members .... 5 minutes

DVD **Top tips for making people feel welcome in church** .... 6 minutes

Community life What goes on at our church? Compiling a list of social events in the church's programme .... 5 minutes

Nurture and pastoral care Discussion of four case studies with reference to nurture and pastoral care .... 10 minutes

DVD Relationships Interview with Sarah Savage .... 7 minutes

Christian service Discussion: does giving them a job keep them or drive them away? .... 5 minutes

Checklists Fill in all five checklists, discuss in pairs or groups then hand in .... 20 minutes

So what did we learn? Sharing ideas and conclusions, announcing checklist results .... 15 minutes

DVD Authors' conclusion .... 2 minutes

Course Prayer .... 2 minutes